CONTENTS

Cornwall

One of the most fascinating areas of the British Isles, Cornwall is a peninsula with its own traditions, language and legends. Here, it is said, King Arthur was born; giants moulded the landscape and smugglers brought ashore their contraband. Today the variety of Cornwall's coastline attracts many holiday makers. The north coast is wild and rugged, its jagged cliffs and jutting headlands battered by the Atlantic rollers. Its old fishing villages are a mecca for artists and its fine beaches and resorts are popular for family holidays. The more gentle south coast is a blend of wooded river estuaries and sandy coves where white-washed stone cottages cluster around tiny harbours. Sub-tropical trees and shrubs grow in profusion in parks and gardens earning Cornwall's southern coast the title of "Cornish Riviera". Inland, the wild solitude of Bodmin Moor, dotted with steep granite tors, is designated an area of outstanding natural beauty.

"A full tide
Rose with ground-swell, on the foremost rocks
Touching, upjetted in spirits of wild sea-smoke."
Alfred Lord Tennyson

Lanyon Quoit

Among the most awe-inspiring and imposing of Cornwall's many ancient monuments are the huge stone burial chambers which were constructed about 4000 years ago. One of the best known is Lanyon Quoit on the Land's End peninsula. It originally stood even taller but it was rebuilt in the early 19th century after suffering a collapse.

Botallack

In the 19th century Cornwall was the centre of an extensive tin and copper mining industry. The county is rich in dramatic ruins which serve as monuments to this heritage, among them the famous Botallack Mine. It has galleries which run beneath the sea, reaching a depth of 1200 feet.

Land's End

Battered by Atlantic waves and gales, the spectacular 200 feet high granite cliffs of Land's End are the most westerly point on the English mainland. Rich in Cornish lore and Celtic legend, this is an area where tales of smuggling and shipwreck are still recounted. Below the cliffs stand the rock formations of Enys Dodman and the Armed Knight, isolated stacks left behind by the retreating sea. Beyond them, the distant Longships Lighthouse warns shipping away from this treacherous coast.

Sennen Cove

Situated at one end of the magnificent sweep of Whitesand Bay is the village of Sennen Cove, England's most westerly community. The little harbour is sheltered below steep slopes and here is housed the lifeboat which is nearest to the wild stretch of coast around Land's End. Tradition has it that King Arthur, leading a group of Cornish chieftains, routed the Danes near here. The spot is marked by a large rock known as the Table Men which stands near Sennen's ancient church.

Porthcurno

Situated on the the wild and rugged Penwith peninsula some three miles from Land's End, is the tiny village of Porthcurno. A place of unsurpassed beauty it is sheltered between two jagged granite headlands which take the force of the constant battering by the winds and waves which break over the off-shore rocks.

Penberth

Described as "the most perfect of Cornish fishing coves", Penberth lies on the southern coast of the Land's End peninsula. Here a few stone-built cottages look out across the rocky shore where fishing boats are drawn up alongside lobster pots and fishing nets. This picturesque and tranquil scene is much loved by artists.

Mousehole

Lying in a valley two miles south of Newlyn is the village of Mousehole which has a long and fascinating history. The tiny harbour is one of the oldest in Cornwall and, despite its size, it was once the county's main fishing port. Fishermen can still be seen landing their catches here and around the snug little harbour quaint old cottages are crowded into the narrow streets.

Penzance

Superbly situated on the wide sweep of Mount's Bay, England's most westerly town has many glorious gardens full of palms, banana trees and other exotic plants which flourish in the exceptionally mild climate. Once Penzance was a major West Country port and the harbour is still a bustling centre of activity. Mainly used by private craft, it is also the point from which the ferry plies between the mainland and the Isles of Scilly.

Mount's Bay

The wide curve of Mount's Bay lies between Land's End and Lizard Point, its rocky shore indented with numerous attractive coves and harbours such as Mousehole and Prussia Cove where this old fisherman's hut stands. Opposite Marazion, one of Cornwall's oldest chartered towns, the rocky pyramid of St. Michael's Mount rises from the sea, crowned by a 14th century castle. A large part of the bay was originally marshy woodland which was submerged in prehistoric times, giving rise to the legend of the lost Land of Lyonesse.

St. Ives

Once one of Cornwall's most prosperous ports, exporting fish as far afield as Italy, the harbour is still at the centre of life in St. Ives. Around it is the old town with its charming colour-washed stone fishermen's cottages crowded together in narrow cobbled streets. Artists have been attracted to St. Ives since the 19th century and the presence of a vibrant artistic community has done much to preserve the character of this ancient fishing port. Now it is internationally known as an artistic centre and a branch of the Tate Gallery opened here in 1993. This is also a popular area with summer visitors who enjoy the fine sandy beaches of St. Ives Bay, the mild climate and the leisurely pursuits of fishing and walking along this fascinating stretch of coast.

"As I was going to St. Ives
I met a man with seven wives . . . ."

Anon

Kynance Cove

Some of the most spectacular scenery on the entire Lizard Peninsula is to be found near rugged Kynance Cove. Here the sea has carved numerous caves and arches in the cliffs which are veined with the purples, reds and greens of the remarkable Serpentine rock. At high tide the swirling sea rushes with dramatic effect through gaps in the rock which are given evocative names like Devil's Letter Box and Bellows. Off shore stand little rocky outcrops known as Gull Rock and Asparagus Island.

"The western wave was all aflame
The day was wellnigh done.
Almost upon the western wave
Rested the broad, bright sun."
Samuel Taylor Coleridge

*"And the stately ships go on
To their haven under the hill."*
Alfred Lord Tennyson

The Lizard

The Lizard Peninsula comprises an infinite variety of scenery. It is known for its majestic coastline, treacherous seas, delightful sandy coves and tiny harbours crowded with boats. Lizard Point is the southernmost extremity of the British mainland and it was here that Cornwall's first lighthouse was built in 1619. It took the form of a coal fire, kept burning to warn sailors away from the rocky coastline which for centuries has been notorious for shipwrecks. Lizard Village, half a mile inland, is a typical Cornish village of sturdy stone-built cottages. It is a good centre for walks and from the Cornwall South Coast Path which traverses the peninsula there are some splendid coastal views.

Cadgwith

One of the most picturesque coves in the county, Cadgwith is a favourite subject for artists. It lies at the foot of a steep and heavily wooded valley between rocky headlands. Small boats still put out from here to fish for crab and lobster and when they are not at sea, the boats are drawn up on to the tiny shingle beach. Many of the ancient fishermen's cottages are built from the local dark green Serpentine stone and there are also some fine examples of the sturdy thatched cottages which abound throughout the Lizard peninsula.

"I love thee Cornwall, and will ever,
And hope to see thee once again.
For why? thine equal knew I never,
For honest minds and active men."
Thomas Freeman

Coverack

The picturesque little fishing village of Coverack lies on the eastern side of the Lizard peninsula under the shelter of Black Head. Complete with its stone-built, whitewashed cottages it is one of the Lizard's most memorable villages. Although it is tiny, the harbour has always provided a vital refuge for the fishermen on this exposed stretch of coast with its dangerous offshore rocks. In past centuries Coverack was also a notorious centre for smuggling.

Frenchman's Creek

One of many beautiful wooded creeks on the Helford River, Frenchman's Creek was made famous by Daphne du Maurier's novel of the same name. Shady paths follow the creek which provides an idyllic setting for walkers and small-boat enthusiasts.

River Fal

Surrounded by scenery of the utmost beauty, the River Fal flows between wooded banks with countless delightful creeks leading off to right and left. When the tides are right it is possible to travel up the river from Falmouth as far as Truro although time spent *en route* wandering along the lovely Mylor and Restronguet creeks rewards the visitor with some delightful byways. The ancient ferry crossing on King Harry Reach is named after Henry VI who swam the river here on horseback. Guarding the Carrick Roads at the entrance to the river are two of the castles built by Henry VIII as part of his coastal defences. Pendennis Castle, which endured a lengthy seige during the Civil War, is notable now for offering superb coastal views. To the east it looks towards St. Mawes Castle with its low central tower surrounded by three bastions.

◁ St. Mawes Castle
Pendennis Castle ▷

Falmouth

Falmouth is a flourishing port with one of the finest natural harbours in the world. Although it had long been a haven for fishing vessels, it was Sir Walter Raleigh who first realised the potential of the Fal estuary as a deep water harbour. The old town is centred around Custom House Quay which was built in the 17th century. As a holiday resort, Falmouth is situated on a superb bay and has a number of good bathing beaches. The town's gardens are filled with sub-tropical plants which flourish in the exceptionally mild climate.

St. Just

Among the charming villages which are scattered throughout the Roseland peninsula is St. Just, providing a peaceful contrast with the busy port of Falmouth on the other side of the Carrick Roads. The pretty little church of St. Just-in-Roseland was built in 1261. Nestling at the water's edge overlooking St. Just Creek, it has one of the most beautiful settings of any church in the country.

Portscatho

Like many other resorts in South Cornwall, Portscatho was originally a quiet fishing village and, with its narrow streets and tiny harbour, it still retains a tranquil atmosphere. It was once an important centre of the mackerel industry but the boats which crowd into the harbour now are mainly used for pleasure. Facing east across Gerrans Bay, Portscatho offers magnificent views towards Nare Head and the isolated stack known as Gull Rock which provides a nesting place for many species of sea bird.

Truro

Cornwall's only city, Truro is situated on the Truro River, an arm of the beautiful Fal estuary. In the Middle Ages it became one of the Stannary towns, active in the Cornish tin mining industry. Its position at the head of the estuary enabled Truro to flourish as a port for many years despite being more than ten miles from the open sea. The cathedral, which stands on the site of an older church, was completed in 1910 in the Early English style.

Veryan

Lying in a sheltered position in a well-wooded valley, the delightful village of Veryan has a mild climate in which sub-tropical trees and plants thrive. The village is known for its unusual Round Houses with their thatched roofs surmounted by a cross. Legend has it that they were built in the Regency period for the five daughters of the vicar and they were round in shape so that there were no corners in which the devil could hide.

Portloe

One of Cornwall's many diminutive ports and harbours, this delightful little fishing village nestles in a steep valley through which a stream runs into the tiny harbour. In the narrow rocky cove there is a slipway which is still used by local fishermen and from the village there are memorable clifftop walks along the Cornwall South Coast Path.

Mevagissey

This picturesque village, protected from the prevailing westerly gales in the shelter of east-facing Mevagissey Bay, was established as a fishing port in the Middle Ages and became an important centre for the pilchard fisheries. The trade has declined in modern times but the colourful inner and outer harbours are still busy with fishing boats and other small craft and the bustling quay is always noisy with the cries of gulls. Sandwiched between steep hills, the harbour is surrounded by narrow streets and twisting alleyways where ancient fishermen's cottages cling precariously to the cliff.

"Pilchards are food,
money and light,
All in one night."

Anon

Heligan

Lying neglected for more than 70 years, the Lost Gardens of Heligan originated in the early years of the 17th century. In an immense and ongoing feat of restoration, these unique and beautiful gardens are now being returned to their former glory, providing a rare opportunity to see the art of the Georgian and Victorian gardener at its best. Among Heligan's many delights are walled gardens, lakes, an Italian garden and a "jungle" area extensively planted with bamboos, palms, tree ferns and other exotic plants.

St. Austell

A prosperous market town with some fine old buildings, St. Austell is a popular touring centre with easy access to the bays and sandy coves of mid-Cornwall. It has been the centre of the china clay industry for nearly 250 years and distinctive white pyramids of china clay waste dominate the landscape around the town. The china clay, or kaolin, which is produced here is of a higher quality than that found anywhere in the world outside China. It is used in the manufacture of many commodities including porcelain, paper, medicines and paint.

Fowey

With its network of narrow streets climbing steeply up from the harbour Fowey is one of the most attractive of Cornwall's ancient coastal towns. It has a long and stirring maritime tradition and during the Hundred Years War the sailors of Fowey, known as "Fowey Gallants", were famous for their ferocity. In times gone by, this deserted stretch of coast at the entrance to the Fowey river was noted for smuggling. The sheltered waters of Fowey's fine natural harbour have made it a busy port since the Middle Ages. An inlet sandwiched between imposing wooded headlands, it provides safe anchorage for hundreds of yachts and Town Quay is always a busy and colourful scene of activity with all manner of craft visiting the town for both business and pleasure. On the other side of the estuary is the ancient little port of Polruan, once a busy ship-building village, and Bodinnick, from where a car ferry plies across the estuary to Fowey. Picturesque old cottages line Bodinnick's breakneck hill as it descends to the ferry slip.

"Many a light fishing-bark
put out to pry along the coast."
Thomas Babington Macauley

Polperro

Situated at the bottom of a deep wooded combe amid outstanding coastal scenery, Polperro is undoubtedly one of England's most enchanting fishing villages. Once notorious for the activities of its smugglers, the tiny, bustling harbour is surrounded by old white-washed cottages, one of which now houses a smuggling museum. Today Polperro provides a safe haven for both fishing boats and pleasure craft. Captured by countless artists and photographers, the tiers of ancient cottages clustered around the harbour convey a timeless sense of peace.

"We left behind the painted buoy
That tosses at the harbour mouth;
And madly danced our hearts with joy
As fast we fleeted to the South."
Alfred Lord Tennyson

Looe

The ancient towns of East and West Looe are built on either side of the deep valley of the Looe River, sandwiched between precipitous hills and linked by an old multi-arched bridge. The harbour is popular with both holiday-makers and fishermen who land their catches, including sharks, at the town's eastern quay. A sandy beach is sheltered by the unusually shaped Banjo Pier and the busy river, which divides into two streams as it wanders inland, is always thronged with small craft.

Whitsand Bay

Deceptively peaceful on a calm day, this four mile long stretch of coast can be treacherous in rough weather when the strong south-westerly winds whip the surf into a frenzy. In the days of sail it was a graveyard for many ships struggling to round Rame Head and reach the shelter of Plymouth Sound.

Saltash

An old town of narrow streets and riverside walks, Saltash is situated on a hill above the River Tamar. It is the historic gateway between Devon and Cornwall, site of a ferry crossing since the 13th century, and now dominated by its two great bridges. The Royal Albert Bridge, which carries the railway across the river, was designed by Brunel and opened by the Prince Consort in 1859.

"Primaeval rocks form the road's steep border,
And much have they faced there, first and last,
Of the transitory in Earth's long order."

Thomas Hardy

Bodmin Moor

The timeless and mysterious atmosphere pervading wild and lonely Bodmin is accentuated by the presence of numerous awe-inspiring ancient monuments. The Hurlers is one of many stone circles which can be found across the moor. Like Stonehenge it is thought to have been used for religious purposes and, according to folklore, the huge granite blocks represent young men turned to stone for breaking the Sabbath by playing ball games – "hurling". The Cheesewring, which stands on the moor not far from Liskeard, is a natural formation of precariously stacked granite blocks. Each stone weighs many tons and the top-most stone is some thirty-four feet in circumference.

Brown Willy

A landscape of contrasts, Bodmin Moor is designated an area of outstanding natural beauty and attracts both naturalists and ramblers with its wild and rugged beauty. Here there is high moorland, bleak and dotted with granite boulders, rolling green hillsides where wild flowers grow in profusion and low marshy ground threaded by streams with bogs which are treacherous to the unwary. Crossed by only one major road and a few lanes, the more remote parts of the moor are only accessible on foot or horseback leaving plenty of secluded areas for the hardy ponies which live wild on Bodmin in all weathers. The moor can boast the highest point in Cornwall, 1,375 feet Brown Willy, and also the source of both the Camel and the Fowey rivers.

Jamaica Inn

Standing in lonely isolation on bleak moorland, often shrouded in mist, Jamaica Inn at Bolventor is redolent with the atmosphere of the 18th century when it was a staging post on the Bodmin to Launceston road for the London mail coach. It is said that smugglers used to store their contraband at the inn which gained enduring fame when Daphne du Maurier used it as the setting for her novel of the same name.

Lanhydrock

Blessed with a gentle climate, Cornwall is rich in superb gardens and great country estates. One of the most outstanding is Lanhydrock, an impressive Jacobean mansion which was largely rebuilt in the 1880s. It stands in 424 acres of parkland overlooking the River Fowey to the south-east of Bodmin. In the midst of the mature trees and rare shrubs which surround the formal garden is the little Church of St. Hydrock.

*"There is nothing -
   absolutely nothing -
half so much worth
   doing as simply messing
about in boats."*

Kenneth Grahame

Lerryn

Several miles upstream from Fowey the river reaches Cliff where it divides into two. The wider branch continues north-west towards Lostwithiel while the beautiful Lerryn River flows to the north and east passing on its way the charming old village of Lerryn. Winding past thickly wooded banks and frequented by heron and curlew, this little stream is without doubt one of the most delightful and attractive parts of the beautiful Fowey estuary. It was a favourite area for the author Kenneth Grahame who indulged his love of boats on the river.

Golitha Falls

The Fowey River rises on Bodmin Moor and as it flows southwards to the sea it passes between the little villages of St. Cleer and St. Neot. Here are the picturesque Golitha Falls where the river tumbles over boulders between wooded banks. They are best reached from Dreynes Bridge where a pleasant woodland walk follows the winding course of the river.

Chapel Porth

Reached by a narrow lane from St. Agnes, the delightful miniature rocky cove of Chapel Porth takes its name from an ancient chapel which once stood in a secluded valley nearby. Situated due south of St. Agnes Head, the beach is backed by steep cliffs with many fine caves to explore and low tide reveals excellent sands. An interesting nature trail takes in the industrial archaeology of the area, left behind by Cornwall's copper and tin mining heritage.

Hayle

From the estuary of the River Hayle to the foot of Godrevy Point the broad sweep of St. Ives Bay is fringed by several miles of sand dunes known as Hayle Towans. A dangerous channel between the point and Godrevy Island claimed many victims until a lighthouse was built in 1859 to warn sailors away from the savage rocks. The novelist Virginia Woolf knew the area well and it was the Godrevy Light which provided the inspiration for her famous novel *To the Lighthouse*.

Perranporth

St. Piran, who gave his name to this popular resort, is said to have sailed from Ireland on a millstone to establish his first church here. St. Piran's Oratory was built in the 6th or 7th century to house the relics of the Celtic saint and, although it was at one time buried beneath the encroaching sands, it can still be seen amid the dunes. Originally a mining village, Perranporth is now known for its magnificent beach which extends for over two miles. Popular for swimming, sunbathing and all the usual activities associated with family seaside holidays, the firm sands are also used out of season for sand yachting. At the southern end of the beach little streams run past the famous Arch and Chapel rocks to the sea.

"By Tre, Pol, and Pen
shall ye know Cornishmen."
Parson R.S.Hawker

Newquay

Although it is Cornwall's largest holiday resort and Britain's main surfing centre, Newquay is an ancient town and the "new quay" from which it takes its name dates from the 15th century. It retains much of its character as an old fishing and trading port and the harbour, which dries out at low tide to provide another beach, is well used by small boats. Built on rocky, granite cliffs, Newquay has a number of caves and many of the sandy beaches are reached by steps or ramps cut into the cliffs.

Constantine

South of rugged Trevose Head is Constantine Bay with its fine sandy beach washed by the surf which rolls in on the Atlantic waves, making this stretch of coastline a favourite with surfers. Behind the beach, the dunes are planted with marram grass to hold up the relentless process of erosion which poses a constant threat for this coastline.

Bedruthan Steps

With its high cliffs and spectacular rock formations Cornwall's Atlantic coast is one of the most memorable stretches in Britain. Legend has it that Bedruthan Steps, detached off-shore rocks created by the action of the sea, were the stepping-stones of a Cornish giant and a steep flight of steps leads down to them from the grassy cliff-top at Carnewas north of Newquay.

Trevose Head

The rocky promontory of Trevose Head thrusts out into the Atlantic, surmounted by a lighthouse which was first erected in 1847. The flat, grassy summit reaches a height of nearly 250 feet above sea level and from the North Cornwall Coast Path which traverses it there are magnificent views along this imposing coastline.

Padstow

With its picturesque little harbour and bustling quayside, Padstow stands on the western side of the broad River Camel estuary. This ancient fishing port is the gateway to some of Cornwall's loveliest bays and the harbour was once one of the busiest on the North Cornwall coast, handling cargoes as diverse as fish, wine, slate and ores. The village is at its most colourful on May Day when the annual 'Obby 'Oss festival takes place to celebrate the coming of summer.

The Camel River

The broad estuary of the River Camel winds inland between grassy cliffs for almost six miles. Flanked by wide stretches of sand, the sheltered waters are always bright with small boats although sand banks present a hazard at low tide. The Camel Trail, which is popular with both walkers and cyclists, follows the course of an abandoned railway line from Wadebridge to Padstow, offering superb views of the estuary. From the mouth of the river a winding, leafy lane leads to the village of Trebetherick where the ancient Church of St. Enodoc has been reclaimed from the sand which at one time threatened to engulf it.

"From Padstow Point to Hartland Light,
is a watery grave both day and night."
Anon

Port Isaac

The tiny haven of Port Isaac, which nestles in a break in the rugged coastline between Padstow and Tintagel, is undoubtedly one of the most picturesque of Cornwall's many fishing villages. Here ancient cottages are squeezed into narrow passageways which cling precariously to the precipitous slopes of one of the steepest hills in Cornwall. An extensive fleet once fished out of Port Isaac and the little harbour, walled in by high cliffs and sheltered from the west by Lobber Point, still provides a welcome haven for fishermen.

Polzeath

Situated at the head of an inlet which opens on to Hayle Bay at the mouth of the Camel estuary, the little resort of Polzeath has a superb expanse of sand. Lying in the shelter of nearby Pentire Point it faces westwards towards Stepper Point, thus benefiting from magnificent sunsets and providing excellent conditions for surfers.

Trebarwith

Less than two miles south of Tintagel, Trebarwith is approached down a steep lane between hillsides which are carpeted with bracken, heather and in spring and early summer, a profusion of wild flowers. The sands extend for nearly a mile and although they are submerged at high tide they are popular with surfers. Sailing ships once called at Trebarwith to trade Welsh coal for slate. Quarried locally, the slate had to be hauled down the cliffs to the boats waiting below. The coal was unloaded into the sea and later, when the tide receded, it was brought ashore by carts. Offshore the bulk of Gull Rock dominates the view seawards.

Tintagel

Situated on the majestic and romantic north-west coast of Cornwall, Tintagel is traditionally associated with the stories of King Arthur and his Knights of the Round Table. Tintagel Castle, perched on the cliffs 300 feet above the sea in an area of breath-taking scenic beauty, was the legendary birthplace of King Arthur. Although the present ruins date only from about 1145, the remains of an ancient Celtic monastery nearby support the theory that the castle was built on the site of an earlier palace which existed in the Dark Ages. On the shore beneath Tintagel Head is Merlin's Cave where the young Arthur is said to have first met the wise wizard. The quaint Old Post Office, situated in Tintagel's main street, is built in the style of a medieval manor house and dates from the 14th century.

"This castle hath a pleasant seat; the air
Nimbly and sweetly recommends itself
Unto our gentle senses."

William Shakespeare

Boscastle

Between the high moors and the stormy seas of this treacherous and rocky coast lies the village of Boscastle with its sturdy cottages clinging to the hillside. Here the tiny River Valency winds through a sheltered valley to the narrow, rock-enclosed harbour which was once busy with sailing ships loading slate from the local mines. Now it provides one of the few refuges from the stormy seas which batter the rugged North Cornwall coast. The novelist Thomas Hardy, who was trained as an architect, met and married his wife at Boscastle while he was doing some restoration work on the Church of St. Juliot.

Morwenstow

This delightful, secluded hamlet lies in a deep combe on the coast and is closely associated with the eccentric theologian and poet, the Reverend R. S. Hawker. Vicar of Morwenstow from 1834 to 1875, he spent much of his time in a hut built from driftwood on the cliff edge. The rectory, which he also built himself, is noted for its chimneys which are replicas of church towers.

Crackington Haven

With its little sand and shingle beach Crackington Haven lies amid spectacular coastal scenery between the towering cliffs of Pencannow Point to the north and Cambeak in the south. On a hill above the Haven is the Church of St. Gennys. In the churchyard are the graves of some of the seafarers whose lives have been claimed by the sea off this dangerous coast.

Penfound Manor

South of the popular surfing resort of Bude stands beautiful Penfound Manor. This mellow old homestead was mentioned in the Domesday Book and is believed to be the oldest inhabited manor house in Britain. Part Saxon and part Norman, with additions made in the Elizabethan and Stuart periods, it represents in one building a microcosm of architectural styles across the ages.

Bude

The most northerly town in Cornwall, Bude was once notorious for the wreckers who looted the many ships which came to grief on the treacherous offshore rocks. To the south nothing impedes the relentless surge of the Atlantic rollers on to the beaches which are popular with surfers from all over the world. Facing west across Bude Bay, this stretch of coast is famous for its spectacular sunsets.

INDEX